M000215135

EVERY DAY
MATTERS
2021 DIARY

A YEAR OF INSPIRATION
FOR THE MIND, BODY & SPIRIT

WATKINS
Sharing Wisdom Since 1893

Every Day Matters 2021 Diary

First published in UK and USA in 2020 by
Watkins, an imprint of Watkins Media Limited
89–93 Shepperton Road, London N1 3DF
enquiries@watkinspublishing.co.uk

Copyright © Watkins Media Limited 2020
Text copyright © Watkins Media Limited 2020
Artwork copyright © Watkins Media Limited 2020

Designed by Watkins Media Limited

Author: Kelly Thompson
Design: Glen Wilkins
Development Editor: Anya Hayes

Desk Diary ISBN: 978-178678-381-3
Pocket Diary ISBN: 978-178678-380-6

Colour reproduction by XY Digital, UK
Printed in China

Phases of the Moon:

● New moon
☽ First quarter
○ Full moon
☾ Last quarter

Signs of the Zodiac:

♒ Aquarius	January 19–February 17
♓ Pisces	February 18–March 19
♈ Aries	March 20–April 18
♉ Taurus	April 19–May 19
♊ Gemini	May 20–June 20
♋ Cancer	June 21–July 21
♌ Leo	July 22–August 21
♍ Virgo	August 22–September 21
♎ Libra	September 22–October 22
♏ Scorpio	October 23–November 21
♐ Sagittarius	November 22–December 20
♑ Capricorn	December 21–January 19

Abbreviations:

BCE: Before Common Era (equivalent of BC)
CE: Common Era (equivalent of AD)
UK: United Kingdom
SCO: Scotland
NIR: Northern Ireland
ROI: Republic of Ireland
CAN: Canada
USA: United States of America
NZ: New Zealand
AUS: Australia
ACT: Australian Capital Territory
NSW: New South Wales
NT: Northern Territory
QLD: Queensland
SA: South Australia
TAS: Tasmania
VIC: Victoria
WA: Western Australia

Publisher's Notes:

All dates relating to the zodiac signs and the
phases of the moon are based on Greenwich
Mean Time (GMT).

All North American holiday dates are based on
Eastern Standard Time (EST).

Jewish and Islamic holidays begin at sundown on
the date given. Islamic holidays may vary by a
day or two, as the Islamic calendar is based on a
combination of actual sightings of the moon and
astronomical calculations.

Note on Public Holidays:

Holiday dates were correct at the time of going
to press.

2020

JANUARY
M	TU	W	TH	F	SA	SU
		1	2	3	4	5
6	7	8	9	10	11	12
13	14	15	16	17	18	19
20	21	22	23	24	25	26
27	28	29	30	31		

FEBRUARY
M	TU	W	TH	F	SA	SU
					1	2
3	4	5	6	7	8	9
10	11	12	13	14	15	16
17	18	19	20	21	22	23
24	25	26	27	28	29	

MARCH
M	TU	W	TH	F	SA	SU
						1
2	3	4	5	6	7	8
9	10	11	12	13	14	15
16	17	18	19	20	21	22
23	24	25	26	27	28	29
30	31					

APRIL
M	TU	W	TH	F	SA	SU
		1	2	3	4	5
6	7	8	9	10	11	12
13	14	15	16	17	18	19
20	21	22	23	24	25	26
27	28	29	30			

MAY
M	TU	W	TH	F	SA	SU
				1	2	3
4	5	6	7	8	9	10
11	12	13	14	15	16	17
18	19	20	21	22	23	24
25	26	27	28	29	30	31

JUNE
M	TU	W	TH	F	SA	SU
1	2	3	4	5	6	7
8	9	10	11	12	13	14
15	16	17	18	19	20	21
22	23	24	25	26	27	28
29	30					

JULY
M	TU	W	TH	F	SA	SU
		1	2	3	4	5
6	7	8	9	10	11	12
13	14	15	16	17	18	19
20	21	22	23	24	25	26
27	28	29	30	31		

AUGUST
M	TU	W	TH	F	SA	SU
					1	2
3	4	5	6	7	8	9
10	11	12	13	14	15	16
17	18	19	20	21	22	23
24	25	26	27	28	29	30
31						

SEPTEMBER
M	TU	W	TH	F	SA	SU
	1	2	3	4	5	6
7	8	9	10	11	12	13
14	15	16	17	18	19	20
21	22	23	24	25	26	27
28	29	30				

OCTOBER
M	TU	W	TH	F	SA	SU
			1	2	3	4
5	6	7	8	9	10	11
12	13	14	15	16	17	18
19	20	21	22	23	24	25
26	27	28	29	30	31	

NOVEMBER
M	TU	W	TH	F	SA	SU
						1
2	3	4	5	6	7	8
9	10	11	12	13	14	15
16	17	18	19	20	21	22
23	24	25	26	27	28	29
30						

DECEMBER
M	TU	W	TH	F	SA	SU
	1	2	3	4	5	6
7	8	9	10	11	12	13
14	15	16	17	18	19	20
21	22	23	24	25	26	27
28	29	30	31			

2021

JANUARY
M	TU	W	TH	F	SA	SU
				1	2	3
4	5	6	7	8	9	10
11	12	13	14	15	16	17
18	19	20	21	22	23	24
25	26	27	28	29	30	31

FEBRUARY
M	TU	W	TH	F	SA	SU
1	2	3	4	5	6	7
8	9	10	11	12	13	14
15	16	17	18	19	20	21
22	23	24	25	26	27	28

MARCH
M	TU	W	TH	F	SA	SU
1	2	3	4	5	6	7
8	9	10	11	12	13	14
15	16	17	18	19	20	21
22	23	24	25	26	27	28
29	30	31				

APRIL
M	TU	W	TH	F	SA	SU
			1	2	3	4
5	6	7	8	9	10	11
12	13	14	15	16	17	18
19	20	21	22	23	24	25
26	27	28	29	30		

MAY
M	TU	W	TH	F	SA	SU
					1	2
3	4	5	6	7	8	9
10	11	12	13	14	15	16
17	18	19	20	21	22	23
24	25	26	27	28	29	30
31						

JUNE
M	TU	W	TH	F	SA	SU
	1	2	3	4	5	6
7	8	9	10	11	12	13
14	15	16	17	18	19	20
21	22	23	24	25	26	27
28	29	30				

JULY
M	TU	W	TH	F	SA	SU
			1	2	3	4
5	6	7	8	9	10	11
12	13	14	15	16	17	18
19	20	21	22	23	24	25
26	27	28	29	30	31	

AUGUST
M	TU	W	TH	F	SA	SU
						1
2	3	4	5	6	7	8
9	10	11	12	13	14	15
16	17	18	19	20	21	22
23	24	25	26	27	28	29
30	31					

SEPTEMBER
M	TU	W	TH	F	SA	SU
		1	2	3	4	5
6	7	8	9	10	11	12
13	14	15	16	17	18	19
20	21	22	23	24	25	26
27	28	29	30			

OCTOBER
M	TU	W	TH	F	SA	SU
				1	2	3
4	5	6	7	8	9	10
11	12	13	14	15	16	17
18	19	20	21	22	23	24
25	26	27	28	29	30	31

NOVEMBER
M	TU	W	TH	F	SA	SU
1	2	3	4	5	6	7
8	9	10	11	12	13	14
15	16	17	18	19	20	21
22	23	24	25	26	27	28
29	30					

DECEMBER
M	TU	W	TH	F	SA	SU
		1	2	3	4	5
6	7	8	9	10	11	12
13	14	15	16	17	18	19
20	21	22	23	24	25	26
27	28	29	30	31		

2022

JANUARY
M	TU	W	TH	F	SA	SU
					1	2
3	4	5	6	7	8	9
10	11	12	13	14	15	16
17	18	19	20	21	22	23
24	25	26	27	28	29	30
31						

FEBRUARY
M	TU	W	TH	F	SA	SU
	1	2	3	4	5	6
7	8	9	10	11	12	13
14	15	16	17	18	19	20
21	22	23	24	25	26	27
28						

MARCH
M	TU	W	TH	F	SA	SU
	1	2	3	4	5	6
7	8	9	10	11	12	13
14	15	16	17	18	19	20
21	22	23	24	25	26	27
28	29	30	31			

APRIL
M	TU	W	TH	F	SA	SU
				1	2	3
4	5	6	7	8	9	10
11	12	13	14	15	16	17
18	19	20	21	22	23	24
25	26	27	28	29	30	

MAY
M	TU	W	TH	F	SA	SU
						1
2	3	4	5	6	7	8
9	10	11	12	13	14	15
16	17	18	19	20	21	22
23	24	25	26	27	28	29
30	31					

JUNE
M	TU	W	TH	F	SA	SU
		1	2	3	4	5
6	7	8	9	10	11	12
13	14	15	16	17	18	19
20	21	22	23	24	25	26
27	28	29	30			

JULY
M	TU	W	TH	F	SA	SU
				1	2	3
4	5	6	7	8	9	10
11	12	13	14	15	16	17
18	19	20	21	22	23	24
25	26	27	28	29	30	31

AUGUST
M	TU	W	TH	F	SA	SU
1	2	3	4	5	6	7
8	9	10	11	12	13	14
15	16	17	18	19	20	21
22	23	24	25	26	27	28
29	30	31				

SEPTEMBER
M	TU	W	TH	F	SA	SU
			1	2	3	4
5	6	7	8	9	10	11
12	13	14	15	16	17	18
19	20	21	22	23	24	25
26	27	28	29	30		

OCTOBER
M	TU	W	TH	F	SA	SU
					1	2
3	4	5	6	7	8	9
10	11	12	13	14	15	16
17	18	19	20	21	22	23
24	25	26	27	28	29	30
31						

NOVEMBER
M	TU	W	TH	F	SA	SU
	1	2	3	4	5	6
7	8	9	10	11	12	13
14	15	16	17	18	19	20
21	22	23	24	25	26	27
28	29	30				

DECEMBER
M	TU	W	TH	F	SA	SU
			1	2	3	4
5	6	7	8	9	10	11
12	13	14	15	16	17	18
19	20	21	22	23	24	25
26	27	28	29	30	31	

Argentina	Jan 1, Feb 15–16, Mar 24, Apr 2, May 1, May 25, Jun 17, Jun 20, Jul 9, Aug 16, Oct 11, Nov 22, Dec 8, Dec 25
Australia	Jan 1, Jan 26, Mar 1 (WA), Mar 8 (ACT, SA, TAS, VIC), Apr 2, Apr 3 (exc TAS, WA), Apr 4, Apr 5, Apr 25, May 3 (NT, QLD), Jun 7 (WA), Jun 14 (exc QLD, WA), Sep 27 (WA), Oct 4 (ACT, NSW, QLD, SA), Dec 25–28
Austria	Jan 1, Jan 6, Apr 5, May 1, May 13, May 24, Jun 3, Aug 15, Oct 26, Nov 1, Dec 8, Dec 25–26
Belgium	Jan 1, Apr 5, May 1, May 13, May 24, Jul 21, Aug 15, Nov 1, Nov 11, Dec 25
Brazil	Jan 1, Apr 2, Apr 21, May 1, Sep 7, Oct 12, Nov 2, Nov 15, Dec 25
Canada	Jan 1, Apr 2, Apr 5, May 24, Jul 1, Sep 6, Oct 11, Nov 11, Dec 24–26
China	Jan 1, Feb 11–17, Apr 5, May 1, Jun 1, Jun 14, Sep 21, Oct 1–7
Denmark	Jan 1, Apr 1–2, Apr 4–5, Apr 30, May 13, May 23–24, Dec 25–26
Finland	Jan 1, Jan 6, Apr 2, Apr 4–5, May 1, May 13, May 23, Jun 25, Nov 6, Dec 6, Dec 24–26, Dec 31
France	Jan 1, Apr 5, May 1, May 8, May 13, May 24, Jul 14, Aug 15, Nov 1, Nov 11, Dec 25
Germany	Jan 1, Apr 2, Apr 5, May 1, May 13, May 24, Oct 3, Dec 25–26
Greece	Jan 1, Jan 6, Mar 15, Mar 25, Apr 30–May 1, May 3, Jun 21, Aug 15, Oct 28, Dec 25–26
India	Jan 26, May 13, Aug 15, Oct 2, Dec 25
Indonesia	Jan 1, Feb 12, Mar 11, Mar 14, Apr 2, May 1, May 13–14, May 26, Jun 1, Jul 20, Aug 10, Aug 17, Oct 19, Dec 25
Israel	Mar 28, Apr 3, Apr 15, May 17, Sep 7–8, Sep 16, Sep 21, Sep 28
Italy	Jan 1, Jan 6, Apr 5, Apr 25, May 1, Jun 2, Aug 15, Nov 1, Dec 8, Dec 25–26
Japan	Jan 1, Jan 11, Feb 11, Feb 23, Mar 20, Apr 29, May 3–5, Jul 19, Aug 11, Sep 20, Sep 23, Oct 11, Nov 3, Nov 23
Luxembourg	Jan 1, Apr 5, May 1, May 9, May 13, May 24, Jun 23, Aug 15, Nov 1, Dec 25–26
Mexico	Jan 1, Feb 1, Feb 5, Mar 15, Mar 21, May 1, Sep 16, Nov 15, Nov 20, Dec 25

Netherlands	Jan 1, Apr 2, Apr 4–5, Apr 27, May 5, May 13, May 23–24, Dec 25–26
New Zealand	Jan 1, Jan 4, Feb 6, Feb 8, Apr 2, Apr 5, Apr 25, Apr 26, Jun 7, Oct 25, Dec 25–28
Nigeria	Jan 1, Apr 2, Apr 5, May 1, May 13–14, Jun 12, Jul 20–21, Oct 1, Oct 19, Dec 25–26
Pakistan	Feb 5, Mar 23, May 1, May 13–16, Jul 20–22, Aug 14, Aug 18–19, Oct 19, Dec 25
Poland	Jan 1, Jan 6, Apr 4–5, May 1, May 3, May 23, Jun 3, Aug 15, Nov 1, Nov 11, Dec 25–26
Portugal	Jan 1, Apr 2, Apr 4, Apr 25, May 1, Jun 3, Jun 10, Aug 15, Oct 5, Nov 1, Dec 1, Dec 8, Dec 25
Republic of Ireland	Jan 1, Mar 17, Apr 5, May 3, Jun 7, Aug 2, Oct 25, Dec 25–26
Russia	Jan 1, Jan 4–8, Feb 23, Mar 8, May 1, May 3, May 9–10, Jun 12, Jun 14, Nov 4
South Africa	Jan 1, Mar 21–22, Apr 2, Apr 5, Apr 27, May 1, Jun 16, Aug 9, Sep 24, Dec 16, Dec 25–27
Spain	Jan 1, Jan 6, Apr 2, May 1, Aug 15–16, Oct 12, Nov 1, Dec 6, Dec 8, Dec 25
Sweden	Jan 1, Jan 6, Apr 2–5, May 1, May 13, May 22–23, Jun 6, Jun 25–26, Nov 6, Dec 24–26, Dec 31
Turkey	Jan 1, Apr 23, May 1, May 14–16, May 19, Jul 15, Jul 20–23, Aug 30, Oct 29
United Kingdom	Jan 1, Jan 4 (SCO), Mar 17 (NIR), Apr 2, Apr 4–5, May 3, May 31, Jul 12 (NIR), Aug 2 (SCO), Aug 30 (exc SCO), Nov 30 (SCO), Dec 25–28
United States	Jan 1, Jan 18, Feb 15, May 31, Jul 4–5, Sep 6, Oct 11, Nov 11, Nov 25, Dec 24–25, Dec 31

WELCOME TO 2021!

Wow! Here we are at the start of a new year, with a fresh chance to take stock of where we are with our life and our dreams, and to choose what we'd like the year ahead to look and feel like for us.

This year, month by month, we encourage you to explore the life-affirming qualities of curiosity, creativity, beauty, loving kindness, authenticity, simplicity, strength, gratitude, connection, mindfulness, joy and growth.

As well as giving you the space to organize your time, this diary – with its vibrant, nature-inspired monthly artworks, thought-provoking weekly quotes and suggestions for inspired action – will motivate you to make every day, week and month the absolute best it can be.

So here's to a year of much beauty, love, connection and joy, filled with days that really matter to you!

CURIOSITY

We can often be so busy focusing on what we have to do and what we already know in life that it's easy to forget just how much new, fascinating stuff there is out there for us to discover. What we don't yet know represents a vast, starry universe of exciting possibilities still to be explored. Let's start off this year by focusing on a range of ways to develop and maintain a playful sense of curiosity every day – like the curiosity that young children inherently enjoy. Looking at the world with fresh eyes means that no matter where you are, who you're with or what you're doing throughout the year ahead, you will always have the capacity to learn, grow and develop a deeper understanding of, and sense of awe for, the incredible world in which we live.

AFFIRMATION OF THE MONTH

Being curious about the world around me allows me to lead a full, rich life

DECEMBER 28 – JANUARY 3
Curiosity

28 / MONDAY

29 / TUESDAY

30 / WEDNESDAY ○

NOTES

> "I think, at a child's birth, if a mother could ask a fairy godmother to endow it with the most useful gift, that gift should be curiosity."

ELEANOR ROOSEVELT (1884–1962), AMERICAN POLITICIAN

31 / THURSDAY
New Year's Eve

1 / FRIDAY
New Year's Day
Kwanzaa ends

2 / SATURDAY

3 / SUNDAY

ASK NEW QUESTIONS

Children are unself-conscious about asking questions to find out about others, but adults can feel anxious about being nosy. Meet a friend and playfully discover three new things about them – a hidden passion, the name of their first love or another new fact. Notice how this curiosity strengthens your bond.

JANUARY 4 – JANUARY 10
Curiosity

4 / MONDAY
Public holiday (SCO, NZ)

5 / TUESDAY

6 / WEDNESDAY ☾
Epiphany

NOTES

> "Minds are like parachutes.
> They only function when open."

SIR JAMES DEWAR (1842–1923), SCOTTISH CHEMIST

7 / THURSDAY
Christmas Day (Orthodox)

8 / FRIDAY

9 / SATURDAY

10 / SUNDAY

OPEN YOUR MIND

Many of us limit our lives in a comfort zone.
But if we open our minds to new experiences,
we'll enjoy more expansiveness in life. This
week, go out of your way to find out about
something outside of your normal experience,
whether a different genre of music, culture or
cuisine, and see how it makes you feel.

JANUARY 11 – JANUARY 17
Curiosity

11 / MONDAY

12 / TUESDAY

13 / WEDNESDAY ●

NOTES

> ## "Be less curious about people and more curious about ideas."

MARIE CURIE (1867–1934), POLISH-FRENCH PHYSICIST

14 / THURSDAY
New Year's Day (Orthodox)

15 / FRIDAY

16 / SATURDAY

17 / SUNDAY

BRAINSTORM POSITIVE IDEAS

When you next find yourself complaining, turn things on their head by being curious about how you could instigate positive change around the situation instead of focusing on the negative. You could even hold a brainstorming session for your friends to share their ideas with you, too.

JANUARY 18 – JANUARY 24
Curiosity

18 / MONDAY
Martin Luther King, Jr Day

19 / TUESDAY ≈

20 / WEDNESDAY ☽

NOTES

> "The real voyage of discovery consists not in seeking new landscapes, but in having new eyes."

MARCEL PROUST (1871–1922), FRENCH AUTHOR

21 / THURSDAY

22 / FRIDAY

23 / SATURDAY

24 / SUNDAY

TAKE A FRESH LOOK

You don't have to travel far to get new perspectives. Look up at the sky and trees the next time you're outside, rather than down at the ground. Really focus on every detail of your food (texture, size, smell, taste...) of your next meal. Looking with fresh eyes at everyday things can provide surprising new insights.

JANUARY 25 – JANUARY 31
Curiosity

25 / MONDAY
Burns Night (SCO)

26 / TUESDAY
Australia Day

27 / WEDNESDAY
International Holocaust
Remembrance Day

NOTES

> "Not till we are lost do we begin to find ourselves."

HENRY DAVID THOREAU (1817–1862), AMERICAN WRITER AND PHILOSOPHER

28 / THURSDAY ○

29 / FRIDAY

30 / SATURDAY

31 / SUNDAY

EMBRACE THE JOURNEY

This week approach any challenge that arises with the passionate curiosity of an adventurer exploring new territory. Set aside any fears of getting a little lost. In going off track, you are likely to make unexpected discoveries – as much about yourself and your own capabilities as about your surroundings.

JANUARY OVERVIEW

M	TU	W	TH	F	SA	SU
28	29	30	31	1	2	3
4	5	6	7	8	9	10
11	12	13	14	15	16	17
18	19	20	21	22	23	24
25	26	27	28	29	30	31

This month I am grateful for . . .

_____

_____

_____

_____

_____

_____

_____

Reflections on CURIOSITY

What new ideas or perspectives did your focus on curiosity lead you to this month?

_____

_____

_____

_____

_____

_____

How did it feel to approach your life with an increased sense of curiosity?

_____

_____

_____

_____

_____

_____

How would you like to continue to stoke the fire of your curiosity moving forward?

_____

_____

_____

_____

_____

_____

FEBRUARY

CREATIVITY

Creativity abounds within each of us. Even if you don't view yourself as a creative person, you innately are. We all have the capacity to create things – from food, conversation and art, to friendships, partnerships and families. As such, you also have the power to continually create the life you want to live. Just as the industrious bee flits from flower to flower, collecting pollen to make honey, so can you consciously choose people, places, beliefs, interactions and experiences in your life that empower and nourish you. There's no need to wait any longer for the "right moment" – when we have more time, more energy, more ideas… Now is the time to recognize and embrace the innate power of creativity within you and use your imagination and resourcefulness to create a month, year and life full of joy, fulfillment and inspiration.

AFFIRMATION OF THE MONTH

*I create the life
I want to live*

FEBRUARY 1 – FEBRUARY 7
Creativity

1 / MONDAY
St Brigid's Day (Imbolc)
Black History Month begins
(CAN, USA)

2 / TUESDAY
Candlemas
Groundhog Day

3 / WEDNESDAY

NOTES

> *"We are what we repeatedly do."*
>
> ARISTOTLE (384–322 BCE), GREEK PHILOSOPHER

4 / THURSDAY ☾

5 / FRIDAY

6 / SATURDAY
Waitangi Day

7 / SUNDAY

START SOMETHING NEW

Think of a good habit you'd like to develop, such as reading for 20 minutes every night or doing a short meditation each morning. Then start carving out the time for this, even if it's just a few minutes a day at first, and then adding more time each day. Soon you'll have created a life-enhancing new habit.

8 / MONDAY
Waitangi Day Holiday
Observed

9 / TUESDAY

10 / WEDNESDAY

NOTES

> "Creativity is not the finding of a thing, but the making something out of it after it is found."

JAMES RUSSELL LOWELL (1819–1891), AMERICAN POET

11 / THURSDAY ●

_____

_____

_____

_____

_____

_____

_____

12 / FRIDAY

Chinese New Year (Year of the Ox)
Abraham Lincoln's birthday
Losar (Tibetan New Year)

_____

_____

_____

_____

_____

_____

13 / SATURDAY

_____

_____

_____

_____

14 / SUNDAY

St Valentine's Day

_____

_____

_____

_____

TURN OLD INTO NEW

Creation isn't only about acquiring or starting something new; it can also be about seeing renewed value in things you already have. This week identify two things that you haven't used in a while: things, skills, contacts, etc. Consider how you might use them to create new experiences and opportunities for yourself.

FEBRUARY 15 – FEBRUARY 21
Creativity

15 / MONDAY
Nirvana Day
Presidents' Day

16 / TUESDAY
Shrove Tuesday

17 / WEDNESDAY
Ash Wednesday

NOTES

> "Every child is an artist. The problem is how to remain an artist once we grow up."

PABLO PICASSO (1881–1973), SPANISH ARTIST

18 / THURSDAY ♓

_____
_____
_____
_____
_____
_____
_____
_____
_____
_____

19 / FRIDAY ☽

_____
_____
_____
_____
_____
_____
_____
_____
_____
_____

20 / SATURDAY

_____
_____
_____
_____

21 / SUNDAY

_____
_____
_____
_____
_____

EMBRACE YOUR INNATE CREATIVITY

Children create in so many ways, from drawing to making up their own games. One evening this week, turn off all your devices and tap into your creative inner child in any way the urge takes you – paint, write, dress up as if you're going to a costume party. And just see how the act of creating makes you feel.

FEBRUARY 22 – FEBRUARY 28
Creativity

22 / MONDAY	23 / TUESDAY	24 / WEDNESDAY

NOTES

> "If you have nothing at all to create,
> then perhaps you create yourself."

CARL GUSTAV JUNG (1875–1961), SWISS PSYCHIATRIST

25 / THURSDAY
Purim begins at sundown

26 / FRIDAY

27 / SATURDAY ○

28 / SUNDAY

CULTIVATE YOUR BEST SELF

Even if you don't view yourself as creative, we each create our daily reality. Each night this week, write down 3 ways you have "created" something, whether a meal, a connection with someone new or a piece of work. Then think of ways in which you could further develop this creative side of your character.

FEBUARY OVERVIEW

M	TU	W	TH	F	SA	SU
1	2	3	4	5	6	7
8	9	10	11	12	13	14
15	16	17	18	19	20	21
22	23	24	25	26	27	28

This month I am grateful for . . .

_____

_____

_____

_____

_____

_____

_____

_____

_____

_____

Reflections on CREATIVITY

In what areas of your life have you recognized creativity this month?

_____

_____

_____

_____

_____

_____

How did it feel to place more focus on creativity in your daily life?

_____

_____

_____

_____

_____

How would you like to continue to nurture your creative side moving forward?

_____

_____

_____

_____

_____

_____

MARCH

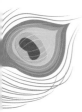

BEAUTY

Beauty comes in all forms – from the sweet song of a lark to the majestic roar of a lion; from the muted hues of a giraffe's patterned skin to the bold, bright colours of a peacock's feathers. But, of course, beauty comes just as much from within as without. Developing the capacity to recognize it in this widest of senses – as more of an emotional response to a wide range of factors than based on external appearance alone – will vastly enhance your experience of the world. It will allow you to look for beauty not as something impossibly "perfect" but as something wondrous in all its imperfection. This will allow you to find beauty in all kinds of unexpected places. And the incredible thing is that the more you look for beauty, the more you will see it. So here's to a beautiful month ahead.

AFFIRMATION OF THE MONTH

I see the beauty in myself and the world around me

MARCH 1 – MARCH 7
Beauty

1 / MONDAY
St David's Day
Labour Day (WA)

2 / TUESDAY

3 / WEDNESDAY

NOTES

> ## "I don't think of all the misery but of the beauty that still remains."

ANNE FRANK (1929–1945), GERMAN DIARIST

4 / THURSDAY
World Book Day

5 / FRIDAY

6 / SATURDAY ☾

---

7 / SUNDAY

LOOK THROUGH AN OPTIMISTIC LENS

There's two ways of looking at things: glass half-empty or glass half-full. The next time something doesn't go the way you had hoped or expected, make a conscious effort to view the glass as half-full by searching for some unexpected beauty in the situation, no matter how minor it might seem at the time.

MARCH 8 – MARCH 14
Beauty

8 / MONDAY
International Women's Day
Commonwealth Day
Public Holiday (ACT, SA,
TAS, VIC)

9 / TUESDAY

10 / WEDNESDAY

NOTES

> "Beauty is not in the face, beauty
> is a light in the heart."

KAHLIL GIBRAN (1883–1931), LEBANESE ARTIST AND WRITER

11 / THURSDAY

12 / FRIDAY

13 / SATURDAY ●

14 / SUNDAY
Daylight Saving Time starts
(CAN, USA)
Mother's Day (UK)

IDENTIFY BEAUTY IN OTHERS

So much of what makes people see others as
beautiful are the positive personality traits that
shine through in their words, mannerisms and
actions rather than anything to do with their
physical looks or stature. Every day this week,
identify two beautiful qualities that you have
noticed in someone that day.

MARCH 15 – MARCH 21
Beauty

15 / MONDAY

16 / TUESDAY

17 / WEDNESDAY
St Patrick's Day

NOTES

> ## "There is no cosmetic for beauty like happiness."

MARGUERITE GARDINER (1789–1849), IRISH NOVELIST

8 / THURSDAY	19 / FRIDAY	20 / SATURDAY ♈
		Spring Equinox (UK, ROI, CAN, USA)
		Autumn Equinox (AUS, NZ)

21 / SUNDAY ☽

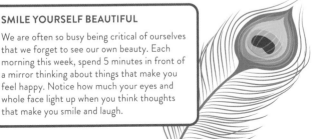

SMILE YOURSELF BEAUTIFUL

We are often so busy being critical of ourselves that we forget to see our own beauty. Each morning this week, spend 5 minutes in front of a mirror thinking about things that make you feel happy. Notice how much your eyes and whole face light up when you think thoughts that make you smile and laugh.

MARCH 22 – MARCH 28
Beauty

22 / MONDAY	23 / TUESDAY	24 / WEDNESDAY

NOTES

> **"Anyone who keeps the ability to see beauty never grows old."**
>
> FRANZ KAFKA (1883-1924), CZECH WRITER

25 / THURSDAY

26 / FRIDAY

27 / SATURDAY
Passover begins at sundown

28 / SUNDAY ○
British Summer Time begins
Palm Sunday

SEE THROUGH CHILDREN'S EYES

Children see the wonder in all sorts of things –
from a line of marching ants to animal shapes
that they can see in clouds. This week, give
yourself permission to be full of this childlike
marvel – look around for unexpected colours,
patterns, shapes and textures and really let
yourself be absorbed by the beauty in them.

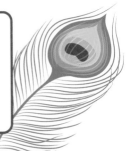

MARCH OVERVIEW

M	TU	W	TH	F	SA	SU
1	2	3	4	5	6	7
8	9	10	11	12	13	14
15	16	17	18	19	20	21
22	23	24	25	26	27	28
29	30	31	1	2	3	4

This month I am grateful for . . .

_____
_____
_____
_____
_____
_____
_____
_____

Reflections on BEAUTY

In what ways did you recognize beauty in your life this month?

_____

_____

_____

_____

_____

_____

How did it feel to pay closer attention to the beauty in everything around you?

_____

_____

_____

_____

_____

Are there any areas of your life in which you'd particularly like to cultivate more of an appreciation of beauty in the future?

_____

_____

_____

_____

_____

APRIL

LOVING KINDNESS

In a world that can sometimes feel tough – and in which many of us are quite harsh on ourselves – making the effort to simply be as kind as possible as we go about our daily business can make a big difference to our experience of life. The more we can act with love and compassion, from the heart, to both ourselves and others in any given situation – instead of getting annoyed, stressed or angry – the less tension and resistance we will feel, and the deeper a sense of connection and peace we will enjoy in body, mind, heart and soul. There are so many ways to share love that it shouldn't be hard to find some that feel comfortable for you already. But this month would be a great time to push yourself outside of your comfort zone, too – to enhance the ripple effect of loving kindness, as it truly is contagious.

AFFIRMATION OF THE MONTH

I treat myself and others with love, kindness and respect each day

MARCH 29 – APRIL 4

Loving kindness

29 / MONDAY
Holi (Festival of Colours)

30 / TUESDAY

31 / WEDNESDAY

NOTES

> "You, yourself, as much as anybody in the entire universe, deserve your love and affection."
>
> GAUTAMA BUDDHA (C. 480–400 BCE)

1 / THURSDAY
April Fools' Day
Maundy Thursday

2 / FRIDAY
Good Friday

3 / SATURDAY
Easter Saturday

4 / SUNDAY ☾
Easter Sunday
Passover ends at sundown

LOVE YOURSELF

Sometimes it can feel more challenging to love ourselves than others. This week make a list of 20 great things about you (maybe the way you bring friends together or the amazing meals you cook). Each time you feel your inner critic emerging, focus on one of these things and say something kind to yourself.

APRIL 5 – APRIL 11
Loving kindness

5 / MONDAY
Easter Monday

6 / TUESDAY

7 / WEDNESDAY

NOTES

> ## "Love is all we have, the only way that each can help the other."

EURIPIDES (C. 480–406 BCE), GREEK POET

8 / THURSDAY	9 / FRIDAY	10 / SATURDAY
		11 / SUNDAY

BE KIND TO STRANGERS

Carrying out random kind acts, however small, is a wonderful way to show loving kindness, even to people we don't know. Every day this week, make it your aim to complete one or more such small acts: hold open a door, give a compliment or help someone carry something.

APRIL 12 – APRIL 18
Loving kindness

12 / MONDAY ●
Ramadan begins at sundown

13 / TUESDAY

14 / WEDNESDAY

NOTES

> ## "Wherever there is a human being, there is an opportunity for kindness."
>
> SENECA (C. 4 BCE–65 CE), ROMAN PHILOSOPHER

5 / THURSDAY	16 / FRIDAY	17 / SATURDAY
_____	_____	_____
_____	_____	_____
_____	_____	_____
_____	_____	_____
_____	_____	**18 / SUNDAY**
_____	_____	_____
_____	_____	_____
_____	_____	_____
_____	_____	_____
_____	_____	_____

LET PEOPLE KNOW YOU SEE THEM

Every interaction you have with someone is an opportunity to show loving kindness. A simple "hello", "thank you", smile or quick chat can change a person's day by making them feel more valued. Make an effort each day this week to acknowledge more people than you normally would in your daily life.

APRIL 19 – APRIL 25
Loving kindness

19 / MONDAY ☿   20 / TUESDAY ☽   21 / WEDNESDAY

NOTES

> "Kind words can be short and easy to speak,
> but their echoes are truly endless."

MOTHER TERESA (1910–1997), MISSIONARY

22 / THURSDAY
Earth Day

23 / FRIDAY
St George's Day

24 / SATURDAY

25 / SUNDAY
Anzac Day

SHARE KIND WORDS

Studies show that we remember negative
experiences more easily than positive ones,
so it takes more positive words to leave a
lasting loving impression. Make a positive
impression this week by leaving a kind message
on a friend's voicemail, or a friendly note of
appreciation for a colleague or family member.

APRIL 26 – MAY 2
Loving kindness

26 / MONDAY	27 / TUESDAY ○	28 / WEDNESDAY

NOTES

> "Love's best habit is a soothing tongue."

WILLIAM SHAKESPEARE (1564–1616) ENGLISH POET AND PLAYWRIGHT

29 / THURSDAY

----

30 / FRIDAY

----

1 / SATURDAY
Beltane

----

2 / SUNDAY
Easter (Orthodox)

SPEAK WITH LOVE

The words we speak are powerful but so, too, is the manner in which those words are spoken. When you speak to others this week, pay close attention to your tone of voice. Is it dismissive or attentive? Sharp or soft? Impatient or kind? Even if your words are positive, is your tone a positive and loving one?

APRIL OVERVIEW

M	TU	W	TH	F	SA	SU
29	30	31	1	2	3	4
5	6	7	8	9	10	11
12	13	14	15	16	17	18
19	20	21	22	23	24	25
26	27	28	29	30	1	2

This month I am grateful for . . .

_____

_____

_____

_____

_____

_____

Reflections on LOVING KINDNESS

In what ways have you added more loving kindness to your life this month?

How has the experience of focusing more on loving kindness made you feel?

In what ways might you like to nurture more loving kindness in the future?

MAY

AUTHENTICITY

What does authenticity really mean? One definition is living in a way that is true to our own nature, values and beliefs. As such, living authentically tends to look different in every individual. The common denominator, however, seems to be a willingness to get to know, accept and love ourselves so that we have the courage to present our most genuine self, flaws and all, to the world around us – like beautiful fern leaves unfurling, each one resplendent in its own uniqueness and perfect imperfection. When we can just be ourselves, rather than trying to be what others around us want or expect, our grounded sense of self will put others at ease and allow deeper connections, joy and fulfillment. So this month, let's see how it feels to really focus our energy on living our most authentic lives.

AFFIRMATION OF THE MONTH

I live each day in tune with my heart's most closely held values

MAY 3 – MAY 9
Authenticity

3 / MONDAY ☾
May Day (NT, QLD)
Early May Bank Holiday
(UK, ROI)

_____

_____

_____

_____

_____

_____

_____

_____

_____

_____

4 / TUESDAY

_____

_____

_____

_____

_____

_____

_____

_____

_____

_____

_____

5 / WEDNESDAY
Cinco de Mayo

_____

_____

_____

_____

_____

_____

_____

_____

_____

_____

_____

NOTES

_____

_____

_____

_____

> "All truths are easy to understand once they are discovered; the point is to discover them."
>
> GALILEO GALILEI (1564–1642), ITALIAN PHYSICIST

6 / THURSDAY   7 / FRIDAY   8 / SATURDAY

9 / SUNDAY
Mother's Day (CAN, USA, AUS, NZ)

IDENTIFY YOUR CORE VALUES

To live in a way that feels true to yourself, it's essential to take the time to get more familiar with your inner world. This week, list seven values that feel important to you: honesty, connection, kindness, growth or whatever else. Each evening, light a candle to honour the place that each one of these has in your life.

MAY 10 – MAY 16

Authenticity

10 / MONDAY	11 / TUESDAY ●	12 / WEDNESDAY
		Ramadan ends at sundown (Eid al-Fitr)

NOTES

> ## "It takes courage to grow up and become who you really are."

E. E. CUMMINGS (1894–1962), AMERICAN POET

3 / THURSDAY
Ascension Day

14 / FRIDAY

15 / SATURDAY

16 / SUNDAY

GET PAST OTHERS' EXPECTATIONS

The expectations of people around us can make it feel tough to live the lives that we know deep down we're meant to live. Write a list of five ways in which you feel held back by how others see you; then write beside each of these one authentic action you can take to help overcome this.

MAY 17 – MAY 23
Authenticity

17 / MONDAY

18 / TUESDAY

19 / WEDNESDAY ☽

NOTES

> "Truth, like gold, is to be obtained not by its growth, but by washing away from it all that is not gold."

LEO TOLSTOY (1828–1910), RUSSIAN NOVELIST

20 / THURSDAY ♊

21 / FRIDAY

22 / SATURDAY

23 / SUNDAY
Pentecost (Whit Sunday)

WASH AWAY THE DIRT

It's important to know who your true friends are in life – the people who you can be your most authentic self with, and who will love you because of this. Think about who has been there for you during your toughest times. Acknowledge these "golden" souls in your life and maybe gently let go of some others.

MAY 24 – MAY 30
Authenticity

24 / MONDAY
Victoria Day (CAN, except NS, NU, QC)

25 / TUESDAY

26 / WEDNESDAY ○

NOTES

> "Between whom there is hearty truth, there is love."

HENRY DAVID THOREAU (1817–1862), AMERICAN WRITER AND PHILOSOPHER

27 / THURSDAY   28 / FRIDAY   29 / SATURDAY

_____   _____   _____
_____   _____   _____
_____   _____   _____
_____   _____   _____
_____   _____   _____
_____   _____   30 / SUNDAY
_____   _____   _____
_____   _____   _____
_____   _____   _____
_____   _____   _____
_____   _____   _____

SPEAK FROM THE HEART

Sometimes the truth can make us feel very
vulnerable. But being truly authentic with
others has the capacity to bring us immensely
closer, as long as it's done in a trusting, loving
space. This week, pluck up the courage to tell a
good friend one deep truth about yourself that
you feel will help them understand you better.

MAY OVERVIEW

M	TU	W	TH	F	SA	SU
26	27	28	29	30	1	2
3	4	5	6	7	8	9
10	11	12	13	14	15	16
17	18	19	20	21	22	23
24	25	26	27	28	29	30
31	1	2	3	4	5	6

This month I am grateful for . . .

_____
_____
_____
_____
_____
_____

Reflections on AUTHENTICITY

In what ways have you sought more authenticity in your life this month?

_____

_____

_____

_____

_____

_____

How has it felt to place more focus on living in a way that is as true to yourself as possible?

_____

_____

_____

_____

_____

_____

Are there areas in your life where you would like to foster more authenticity moving forward?

_____

_____

_____

_____

_____

_____

JUNE

SIMPLICITY

Modern life is busy, and the busier it gets, the more frazzled we can feel. With stress and anxiety levels on the rise, it's more important than ever that we take time to recognize that life doesn't always have to be as full and complex as we often make it – in terms of our time commitments, belongings, emotions and everything else. It is, after all, within our own power to be more discerning about what we choose to give our time and energy to. This month let's consider ways in which we can start to simplify things for ourselves, to free up more time, space and energy to enjoy the little things in life more – whether this is holding your partner's hand or lying in a field of wildflowers and just soaking up the wonder of nature. There is much beauty to be found in simplicity.

AFFIRMATION OF THE MONTH

I seek simplicity in all things

31 / MONDAY	1 / TUESDAY	2 / WEDNESDAY ☾
Spring Bank Holiday (UK)		
Memorial Day (USA)		

NOTES

> "I am beginning to learn that it is the sweet, simple things of life which are the real ones after all."

LAURA INGALLS WILDER (1867–1957), AMERICAN WRITER

3 / THURSDAY

4 / FRIDAY

5 / SATURDAY

6 / SUNDAY

NOTICE THE SIMPLE THINGS

Moments of simple delight can often pass so quietly that we don't stop to appreciate them. Each day this week identify one simple act that makes you feel contented – freshly squeezed morning juice, watching the sun set, catching up with an old friend – and take the time to appreciate its simple beauty.

JUNE 7 – JUNE 13
Simplicity

7 / MONDAY
June Bank Holiday (ROI)
Queen's birthday celebrated (NZ)
Western Australia Day (WA)

8 / TUESDAY

9 / WEDNESDAY

NOTES

> "Have nothing in your houses that you do not know to be useful or believe to be beautiful."

WILLIAM MORRIS (1834–1896), BRITISH TEXTILE DESIGNER AND WRITER

10 / THURSDAY ●　　**11 / FRIDAY**　　**12 / SATURDAY**

---

13 / SUNDAY

CLEANSE YOUR SPACE

It's all too easy for our homes to become overly full and cluttered. To make things feel lighter, choose one cupboard each night this week and work your way through each item in it, asking yourself: do I use it regularly? And does it give me joy? If the answer to both is no, why not sell it or pass it on to charity?

14 / MONDAY

Queen's birthday celebrated
(AUS, except QLD, WA)

15 / TUESDAY

16 / WEDNESDAY

NOTES

> "The art of being wise is the art
> of knowing what to overlook."

WILLIAM JAMES (1842–1910), AMERICAN PHILOSOPHER

17 / THURSDAY	18 / FRIDAY ☽	19 / SATURDAY
		20 / SUNDAY
		Father's Day (UK, ROI, CAN, USA)

TAKE A WIDER VIEW

Modern life can be an overwhelming
bombardment of demands on our time. One
night this week, sit quietly, close your eyes and
visualize yourself taking a step back from it all
to get a wider view of what really matters in
your life. Feel where you need to focus your
energy and what you can let go of.

JUNE 21 – JUNE 27
Simplicity

21 / MONDAY ♋
Summer Solstice (UK, ROI, CAN, USA)
Winter Solstice (AUS, NZ)

22 / TUESDAY

23 / WEDNESDAY

NOTES

> "Beware the barrenness of a busy life."

SOCRATES (469–399 BCE), GREEK PHILOSOPHER

24 / THURSDAY ○   **25 / FRIDAY**   **26 / SATURDAY**

_____   _____   _____
_____   _____   _____
_____   _____   _____
_____   _____   _____
_____   _____
_____   _____   **27 / SUNDAY**
_____   _____   _____
_____   _____   _____
_____   _____   _____
_____   _____   _____
_____   _____   _____

FREE UP SOME TIME

One day this week clear your diary of all
non-essentials. Be firm – cancel unnecessary
errands, postpone unimportant meetings,
respond only to urgent messages. Use the time
to savour life's essentials – bathing, eating,
exercising, sleeping, loving – and observe how
enriching each of these acts can feel.

JUNE OVERVIEW

M	TU	W	TH	F	SA	SU
31	1	2	3	4	5	6
7	8	9	10	11	12	13
14	15	16	17	18	19	20
21	22	23	24	25	26	27
28	29	30	1	2	3	4

This month I am grateful for . . .

_____

_____

_____

_____

_____

_____

Reflections on SIMPLICITY

In what ways did you bring more simplicity into your life this month?

_____

_____

_____

_____

_____

_____

How did it feel to focus on simplifying certain aspects of your life?

_____

_____

_____

_____

_____

_____

What further strategies could you put in place to continue to make life feel simpler?

_____

_____

_____

_____

_____

_____

JULY

STRENGTH

One definition of the word strength is the ability to withstand a lot of either physical or mental exertion. A good dose of strength – both inward (of mind and heart) and outward (of body) – is therefore a desirable quality in all of us, as it gives us the skill to cope better with life's many challenges, whether physical, mental or emotional. From the outset, it's important to set aside any outdated notions of strength being about machismo and toughness. Instead, this month we will explore a more nuanced notion of strength – one as much about openness and softness as traditional toughness and bravery. If we can learn to be like strong, sturdy trees, with our roots firmly planted in the earth, our branches free and flexible to move with the ever-changing wind, then we will thrive. So, here's to a month of recognizing and reclaiming our existing strengths, as well as developing some new ones.

AFFIRMATION OF THE MONTH

I embrace the strength that lies within me

JUNE 28 – JULY 4
Strength

28 / MONDAY	29 / TUESDAY	30 / WEDNESDAY

NOTES

> "You have power over your mind – not outside events. Realize this, and you will find strength."

MARCUS AURELIUS (121–180 CE), ROMAN EMPEROR AND PHILOSOPHER

/ THURSDAY ☾
Canada Day

2 / FRIDAY

3 / SATURDAY

4 / SUNDAY
Independence Day (USA)

SET YOUR MIND UP FOR THE DAY

Spend 10–15 minutes each morning writing a stream-of-consciousness in a notebook as soon as you get up, without pausing to self-correct or reread your words. This process helps to cleanse your mind of distracting, potentially unhelpful thoughts and worries, leaving it clearer and stronger for the day ahead.

JULY 5 – JULY 11
Strength

5 / MONDAY
Independence Day observed (USA)

_____

_____

_____

_____

_____

_____

_____

_____

_____

_____

_____

_____

6 / TUESDAY

_____

_____

_____

_____

_____

_____

_____

_____

_____

_____

_____

_____

7 / WEDNESDAY

_____

_____

_____

_____

_____

_____

_____

_____

_____

_____

_____

_____

NOTES

_____

_____

_____

_____

> "You gain strength, courage and confidence by every experience in which you really stop to look fear in the face."

ELEANOR ROOSEVELT (1884–1962), AMERICAN POLITICIAN

8 / THURSDAY

.

9 / FRIDAY

10 / SATURDAY ●

11 / SUNDAY

WELCOME YOUR FEARS

Your fears are opportunities to find your reserves of inner strength. Pick a day this week to do something you've been afraid to do – ask for a payrise, book in a skydive or tell someone you love them. Once you've conquered one fear – no matter how small – you'll find more strength to tackle others.

JULY 12 – JULY 18
Strength

12 / MONDAY
Orangemen's Day (NIR)

13 / TUESDAY

14 / WEDNESDAY
Bastille Day

NOTES

> ## "Out of suffering have emerged the strongest souls."
>
> KAHLIL GIBRAN (1883–1931), LEBANESE ARTIST AND WRITER

15 / THURSDAY   16 / FRIDAY   17 / SATURDAY »

18 / SUNDAY

LOOK FOR STRENGTH IN HARD TIMES

Events that we might consider as tragedies or failures at the time can often lead us to great things. Think of something you feel went wrong for you in the past. Consider what you learned from the experience and how the learning – as well as the resilience you gained – has become, or could become, a valuable strength.

JULY 19 – JULY 25
Strength

19 / MONDAY
Eid al-Adha (Feast of the Sacrifice) begins at sundown

20 / TUESDAY

21 / WEDNESDAY

NOTES

> "It is good to love many things, for therein lies the true strength, and whosoever loves much performs much, and can accomplish much."

VINCENT VAN GOGH (1853–1890), DUTCH PAINTER

22 / THURSDAY ♌   **23 / FRIDAY**   **24 / SATURDAY** ○

---

25 / SUNDAY

MAKE LOVE A PRIORITY IN YOUR LIFE

Incredible strength is found in love. The experience of a heartfelt connection with people, places, activities and things reminds us that we are not alone and bolsters our sense of belonging and purpose. One night this week, list ten passions, noticing how you gain strength from each of these in different ways.

JULY 26 – AUGUST 1
Strength

26 / MONDAY	27 / TUESDAY	28 / WEDNESDAY

NOTES

> "Blessed are the hearts that can bend;
> they shall never be broken."

ALBERT CAMUS (1913–1960), FRENCH-ALGERIAN PHILOSOPHER AND WRITER

29 / THURSDAY

30 / FRIDAY

31 / SATURDAY ☾

1 / SUNDAY

ENHANCE YOUR EMOTIONAL AGILITY

Emotional agility is important to improve
your mental resilience. If you feel emotionally
"stuck", visualize yourself as a tree grounded in
the earth with strong roots, with your branches
(your thoughts and emotions) gracefully
swaying in the wind not rigidly resisting it.
Observe how this makes you feel.

JULY OVERVIEW

M	TU	W	TH	F	SA	SU
28	29	30	1	2	3	4
5	6	7	8	9	10	11
12	13	14	15	16	17	18
19	20	21	22	23	24	25
26	27	28	29	30	31	1

This month I am grateful for . . .

Reflections on STRENGTH

In what ways have you recognized your own strengths this month?

_____

_____

_____

_____

_____

_____

How did it feel to think about what the word strength really means to you?

_____

_____

_____

_____

_____

Are there specific ways in which you would like to develop more strength in the future?

_____

_____

_____

_____

_____

_____

AUGUST

GRATITUDE

Gratitude is recognition and expression of appreciation for all that we are lucky enough to have – whether tangible, such as delicious fresh bounty from nature, or intangible, such as a sense of inner calm on a hectic working day. A regular gratitude practice has now been scientifically proven to reduce negative emotions such as frustration, anger, stress and regret, as well as enhancing positive ones such as empathy, happiness, motivation and self-esteem. The best way to reap the benefits of gratitude is to take note in a journal every night of new things you're thankful for, as this will slowly adjust the focus of the lens through which you see life. It may feel contrived at first, but you will soon start feeling positive ripples throughout your life.

AFFIRMATION OF THE MONTH

I am deeply grateful for all that I have and all that I am

AUGUST 2 – AUGUST 8
Gratitude

2 / MONDAY
August Bank Holiday (ROI, SCO)

3 / TUESDAY

4 / WEDNESDAY

NOTES

> "Do not spoil what you have by desiring what you have not."

EPICTETUS (C. 55–135 CE), GREEK PHILOSOPHER

5 / THURSDAY	6 / FRIDAY	7 / SATURDAY
		8 / SUNDAY ●

APPRECIATE WHAT YOU HAVE

Always wanting more – time, energy, happiness, money – is missing appreciating what we already have. This week, list five things you are grateful for. Pin it up somewhere obvious; on the fridge or bathroom mirror. If you catch yourself wishing for more, glance at it, smile and allow yourself to be thankful.

AUGUST 9 – AUGUST 15
Gratitude

9 / MONDAY
Islamic New Year (first day
of Muharram) begins at
sundown

10 / TUESDAY

11 / WEDNESDAY

NOTES

> "We often take for granted the very things
> that most deserve our gratitude."

CYNTHIA OZICK (1928–), AMERICAN WRITER

12 / THURSDAY	13 / FRIDAY	14 / SATURDAY
		15 / SUNDAY ☽

SAVOUR THE ESSENTIALS

As well as being thankful for all our modern
luxuries, it's important to be grateful for basics
such as clean water and essential food, which
so many people around the world aren't lucky
enough to have. Consider donating your time
or money to a charity that helps the less
fortunate access these basic needs.

AUGUST 16 – AUGUST 22
Gratitude

16 / MONDAY

17 / TUESDAY

18 / WEDNESDAY

NOTES

> "Feeling gratitude and not expressing it is like wrapping a present and not giving it."

WILLIAM ARTHUR WARD (1921-1994), AMERICAN WRITER

19 / THURSDAY	20 / FRIDAY	21 / SATURDAY

22 / SUNDAY ♍ ○

OUTWARDLY GIVE THANKS

As well as developing an inner attitude of gratitude by keeping a daily gratitude journal, it's important to outwardly show how thankful we are to people who support us. This week, choose one person you are thankful to have in your life and acknowledge them in some small way, such as sending them a card or flowers.

AUGUST 23 – AUGUST 29
Gratitude

23 / MONDAY

24 / TUESDAY

25 / WEDNESDAY

NOTES

> "Gratitude is not only the greatest of virtues, but the parent of all others."

MARCUS TULLIUS CICERO (106–43 BCE), ROMAN PHILOSOPHER

26 / THURSDAY   27 / FRIDAY   28 / SATURDAY

_____   _____   _____
_____   _____   _____
_____   _____   _____
_____   _____   _____
_____   _____

_____   _____   29 / SUNDAY

_____   _____   _____
_____   _____   _____
_____   _____   _____
_____   _____   _____
_____   _____

NOTICE WHAT GRATITUDE LEADS TO

The practice of gratitude lays a foundation
for many other positive behaviours, such as
kindness, humility and compassion. Each night
this week, consider how your gratitude might
ripple out positively. Perhaps gratitude for your
healthy children might give you more patience
with them, and so on.

AUGUST OVERVIEW

M	TU	W	TH	F	SA	SU
26	27	28	29	30	31	1
2	3	4	5	6	7	8
9	10	11	12	13	14	15
16	17	18	19	20	21	22
23	24	25	26	27	28	29
30	31	1	2	3	4	5

This month I am grateful for . . .

_____

_____

_____

_____

_____

_____

Reflections on GRATITUDE

In what areas of your life did you notice a newfound sense of gratitude this month?

How did it feel to put a particular emphasis on being grateful for what you have?

Do you feel it would be useful to develop gratitude in other aspects of your life as the year unfolds? If so, in what aspects?

CONNECTION

Like everything else in nature, our human lives are intricately connected with the lives of those around us. We are all linked through energy, information, ideas, thoughts and beliefs that we gather as we move through the world. These connections have the potential to strengthen or transform us if we keep our minds and hearts open. Let's focus this month on exploring the many connections that we have the chance to tap into – whether that's a deeper connection with ourselves, our families, friends old and new, our local community, or the planet. Becoming more aware of these multiple levels of connection enhances our understanding, and enjoyment, of our daily lives. Here's to a month of feeling more connected...

AFFIRMATION OF THE MONTH

I feel a sense of deep connection with the world around me

AUGUST 30 – SEPTEMBER 5
Connection

30 / MONDAY ☾
Summer Bank Holiday (UK, except SCO)

31 / TUESDAY

1 / WEDNESDAY

NOTES

> "In nature we never see anything isolated, but everything in connection with something else."

JOHANN WOLFGANG VON GOETHE (1749–1832), GERMAN WRITER

2 / THURSDAY	3 / FRIDAY	4 / SATURDAY
		5 / SUNDAY
		Father's Day (AUS, NZ)

RECONNECT WITH NATURE

If ever you're feeling lonely or in need of a boost, step outside and observe nature – birds singing or in flight, ants working together, spiders creating their wondrous webs – to be reminded of the interconnectedness of all living things. Take a moment to remind yourself that you, too, are part of this one ecosystem.

SEPTEMBER 6 – SEPTEMBER 12
Connection

6 / MONDAY
Labor Day (CAN, USA)
Rosh Hashanah (Jewish New Year) begins at sundown

7 / TUESDAY ●

8 / WEDNESDAY

NOTES

> "Connection and connectedness are other words for community and communion."

PARKER J. PALMER (1939–), AMERICAN AUTHOR AND EDUCATOR

9 / THURSDAY

10 / FRIDAY

11 / SATURDAY

12 / SUNDAY

CONTRIBUTE TO YOUR COMMUNITY

It's easy to get absorbed in looking after your own family's needs and wants. This week, offer something to your wider community – volunteer for a charity or local initiative, such as a beach clean-up. See how it feels to be more connected, not just with other people in your area, but also to a common cause.

SEPTEMBER 13 – SEPTEMBER 19
Connection

13 / MONDAY ☽

14 / TUESDAY

15 / WEDNESDAY
Yom Kippur (Day of
Atonement) begins at
sundown

NOTES

> "Invisible threads are the strongest ties."

FRIEDRICH NIETZSCHE (1844–1900), GERMAN PHILOSOPHER

16 / THURSDAY

_____
_____
_____
_____

_____

_____
_____
_____
_____
_____

17 / FRIDAY

_____
_____
_____
_____

_____

_____
_____
_____
_____
_____

18 / SATURDAY

_____
_____
_____
_____

19 / SUNDAY

_____
_____
_____
_____
_____

LOOK BELOW THE SURFACE

It's not only your obvious connections who enrich your life. Notice this week how many others add to the tapestry of your days – the guy who serves you coffee each morning, or old friends who get in touch occasionally by text. Take the time to really acknowledge the value of these people in your life.

SEPTEMBER 20 – SEPTEMBER 26

Connection

20 / MONDAY

Sukkot (Feast of the Tabernacles) begins at sundown

21 / TUESDAY ○

International Day of Peace

22 / WEDNESDAY ◿

Autumn Equinox (UK, ROI, CAN, USA)
Spring Equinox (AUS, NZ)

NOTES

> "Mindfulness practices enhance the connection between our body, our mind and everything else that is around us."

THICH NHAT HANH (1926–), VIETNAMESE MONK

23 / THURSDAY   24 / FRIDAY   25 / SATURDAY

_____

26 / SUNDAY

CONNECT WITH YOURSELF

It's vital to take time out to reconnect with yourself as well as the world around you. Your breath is the perfect vehicle for this. If things get hectic this week, spend 2 minutes just observing your breath as it comes in through your nose, then out through your mouth. Do you feel more grounded?

SEPTEMBER OVERVIEW

M	TU	W	TH	F	SA	SU
30	31	1	2	3	4	5
6	7	8	9	10	11	12
13	14	15	16	17	18	19
20	21	22	23	24	25	26
27	28	29	30	1	2	3

This month I am grateful for . . .

Reflections on CONNECTION

In what ways have you experienced a stronger sense of connection with yourself and the world around you this month?

_____

_____

_____

_____

_____

How did it feel to explore bringing a deeper sense of connection into your life?

_____

_____

_____

_____

_____

Are there any particular areas of your life in which you'd like to further enhance your sense of connection?

_____

_____

_____

_____

_____

OCTOBER

MINDFULNESS

With origins in Buddhist meditation, the practice of mindfulness – cultivating a non-judgmental awareness of the present moment – is as accessible and valuable for modern humans now as it has been for millennia. When we choose to gently place our focus on one thing – an object, our breath, our body, a sensory experience – the often turbulent waters of our mind are invited to slow down and find stillness. Only then can the beautiful lotus flowers growing be seen more clearly on the surface. Stillness is not a lack of thoughts and emotions; mindfulness is not emptying your mind but simply allowing the thoughts and emotions to "be". So this month, let's enjoy bringing more mindfulness into our daily lives in a range of ways.

AFFIRMATION OF THE MONTH

I bring a mindful quality into everything I do

SEPTEMBER 27 – OCTOBER 3
Mindfulness

27 / MONDAY
Public holiday (WA)

28 / TUESDAY

29 / WEDNESDAY ☾

NOTES

> ## "You are the sky.
> ## Everything else is just the weather."

PEMA CHÖDRÖN (1936–), AMERICAN BUDDHIST TEACHER

30 / THURSDAY	1 / FRIDAY	2 / SATURDAY
	Black History Month begins (UK)	

3 / SUNDAY

VIEW YOUR THOUGHTS LIKE CLOUDS IN THE SKY

We are not our thoughts. We have the power to observe our thoughts, and choose which ones to give our attention to. Visualize thoughts as clouds in the sky: you can simply observe them float on, rather than allowing them to linger and rain or create thunder!

OCTOBER 4 – OCTOBER 10
Mindfulness

4 / MONDAY
Public holiday (ACT, NSW, QLD, SA)

5 / TUESDAY

6 / WEDNESDAY ●

NOTES

> ## "Nothing is worth more than this day."
>
> JOHANN WOLFGANG VON GOETHE (1749–1832), GERMAN POET

7 / THURSDAY	8 / FRIDAY	9 / SATURDAY
		10 / SUNDAY

MINDFULLY CHOOSE YOUR THOUGHTS

Our thoughts create our reality so it's worth being mindful of what we are creating. This week use the TAP method to pay attention. If you feel self-judgment creeping in, ask yourself: Is this thought **T**rue? Is it **A**dding value? Is it **P**ositive? If the thought doesn't meet those three criteria, try to let it go.

OCTOBER 11 – OCTOBER 17
Mindfulness

11 / MONDAY
Thanksgiving (CAN)
Indigenous Peoples' Day/
Columbus Day

12 / TUESDAY

13 / WEDNESDAY 》

NOTES

> "With the past, I have nothing to do;
> nor with the future. I live now."

RALPH WALDO EMERSON (1803–1882), AMERICAN ESSAYIST

14 / THURSDAY   15 / FRIDAY   16 / SATURDAY

17 / SUNDAY

TUNE INTO YOUR SENSES

Our senses connect us directly to the present
moment. This week notice a daily sense,
perhaps sight on Monday, hearing on Tuesday
and so on. Whenever you become distracted,
tune into that sense and focus on what you're
experiencing through it, allowing yourself to be
fully immersed in the current experience.

OCTOBER 18 – OCTOBER 24
Mindfulness

18 / MONDAY
Milad un-Nabi (Sunni;
birthday of the Prophet
Muhammed) begins at
sundown

19 / TUESDAY

20 / WEDNESDAY ○

NOTES

> "Be where you are; otherwise
> you will miss your life."

GAUTAMA BUDDHA (C. 480-400 BCE)

21 / THURSDAY

22 / FRIDAY

23 / SATURDAY ♏

24 / SUNDAY

MAKE EACH ACTION MINDFUL

Each time you eat or drink something this
week, give it your full attention, chewing or
sipping it mindfully. Ignore other demands: it's
just you and the food or drink in this moment.
Give other activities your full deliberate
attention in the same way, whether cooking a
meal, doing the washing up or anything else.

OCTOBER 25 – OCTOBER 31
Mindfulness

25 / MONDAY
Labour Day (NZ)
October Bank Holiday
(ROI)

26 / TUESDAY

27 / WEDNESDAY

NOTES

> "The idea of meditation is not to create states of ecstasy, but to experience being."

CHÖGYAM TRUNGPA (1939–1987), BUDDHIST MEDITATION MASTER

28 / THURSDAY ☾

---

29 / FRIDAY

---

30 / SATURDAY

---

31 / SUNDAY
Halloween
Samhain
British Summer Time ends

MINDFULLY SCAN YOUR BODY

In a quiet space, lie with your hands relaxed by your sides. Take slow, deep breaths. Bring your attention first to your head and neck, noticing any sensations, softening into them. Then, scan all other areas of your body in a similar way, from your head down to your toes. Do you feel more grounded and connected to your body?

OCTOBER OVERVIEW

M	TU	W	TH	F	SA	SU
27	28	29	30	1	2	3
4	5	6	7	8	9	10
11	12	13	14	15	16	17
18	19	20	21	22	23	24
25	26	27	28	29	30	31

This month I am grateful for . . .

Reflections on MINDFULNESS

Have you had any fresh insights into the concept of mindfulness this month? If so, what?

_____

_____

_____

_____

_____

_____

How has it made you feel to place more of a focus on mindfulness in your everyday life?

_____

_____

_____

_____

_____

_____

Are there any particular ways that you would like to develop mindfulness more in the future?

_____

_____

_____

_____

_____

Don't miss out on next year's diary! See the back page
for details on how to order your copy for 2022.

NOVEMBER

JOY

When we're happy and joyous, it feels like the sun is shining down on us, warming our faces, soothing our souls and lifting our hearts. Who doesn't want more of that positive feeling in their lives? Let's focus our energy this month on injecting more of this experience into our days by exploring where and when you get the most joy as you go about your daily business, what this means to you and different ways to access more of the same. Often the very act of being aware of something will bring more of it into our lives. Wouldn't it be wonderful if this were to happen in our search for more happiness and joy. Bring on the joy!

AFFIRMATION OF THE MONTH

I seek joy in everything I do

NOVEMBER 1 – NOVEMBER 7

Joy

1 / MONDAY
All Saints' Day

2 / TUESDAY
All Souls' Day

3 / WEDNESDAY

NOTES

> ## "Joy in looking and comprehending is nature's most beautiful gift."

ALBERT EINSTEIN (1879–1955), GERMAN THEORETICAL PHYSICIST

4 / THURSDAY ●
Diwali

5 / FRIDAY

6 / SATURDAY

7 / SUNDAY
Daylight Saving Time ends
(CAN, USA)

ENJOY THE VIEW

This week, take delight in paying attention
to your surroundings everywhere you go –
whether in relation to places, people, events,
interactions, and so on. Be aware of the things
that give you the most joy, and consider why
you think this is, so that you can look for more
such "joy triggers" elsewhere in your life.

NOVEMBER 8 – NOVEMBER 14

Joy

8 / MONDAY	9 / TUESDAY	10 / WEDNESDAY

NOTES

> "Sometimes your joy is the source of your smile, but sometimes your smile can be the source of your joy."

THICH NHAT HANH (1926–), VIETNAMESE MONK

11 / THURSDAY ☽
Veterans Day (USA)
Remembrance Day (CAN)

12 / FRIDAY

13 / SATURDAY

14 / SUNDAY
Remembrance Sunday (UK)

SMILE FROM THE INSIDE OUT

Feeling happy is the ultimate joy in a healthy life. Try the practice of inner smiling – particularly when you find yourself in difficult situations. Gently smiling on the inside, no matter what happens around you, allows you to observe your thoughts and emotions rather than them being in control of you.

NOVEMBER 15 – NOVEMBER 21

Joy

15 / MONDAY

16 / TUESDAY

17 / WEDNESDAY

NOTES

> "I would always rather be happy than dignified."

CHARLOTTE BRONTË (1816–1855), ENGLISH NOVELIST

18 / THURSDAY

_____
_____
_____
_____
_____
_____
_____
_____
_____
_____

19 / FRIDAY ○

_____
_____
_____
_____
_____
_____
_____
_____
_____
_____

20 / SATURDAY

_____
_____
_____
_____

21 / SUNDAY
World Hello Day

_____
_____
_____
_____
_____

EMBRACE YOUR SILLY SIDE

The most joyous times can be found when we
are free from caring what others think. This
week, mimic a small child's lack of inhibitions –
choose to embrace joy by doing one silly thing
each day – skip along the pavement, dance
around, make funny faces in the mirror, or
anything else that tickles your fancy.

NOVEMBER 22 – NOVEMBER 28

Joy

22 / MONDAY ♐   23 / TUESDAY   24 / WEDNESDAY

_____   _____   _____
_____   _____   _____
_____   _____   _____
_____   _____   _____
_____   _____   _____
_____   _____   _____
_____   _____   _____
_____   _____   _____
_____   _____   _____
_____   _____   _____
_____   _____   _____
_____   _____   _____

NOTES

_____
_____
_____

> ## "A great obstacle to happiness is to expect too much happiness."

BERNARD LE BOVIER DE FONTENELLE (1657–1757), FRENCH AUTHOR

25 / THURSDAY	26 / FRIDAY	27 / SATURDAY ☾
Thanksgiving Day (USA)		

28 / SUNDAY
First Sunday of Advent
Hanukkah begins at sundown

SET FREE YOUR EXPECTATIONS

Expecting a certain outcome carries with it the potential for frustration. Each morning this week, consider your expectations for the day. Pick one and challenge it with this mantra: Whatever the result, I will be happy. If you feel the desire for an expected outcome creeping back in, repeat the mantra and let the expectation go.

NOVEMBER OVERVIEW

M	TU	W	TH	F	SA	SU
1	2	3	4	5	6	7
8	9	10	11	12	13	14
15	16	17	18	19	20	21
22	23	24	25	26	27	28
29	30	1	2	3	4	5

This month I am grateful for . . .

Reflections on JOY

Have you experienced more joy this month? If so, in what ways?

_____

_____

_____

_____

_____

_____

How has it felt to consciously seek more joy in your life?

_____

_____

_____

_____

_____

In what ways might you like to add more joy to your life in the future?

_____

_____

_____

_____

_____

_____

DECEMBER

GROWTH

Here we are near the end of the year already! What better time to take stock of how much you have grown through all the events, both fulfilling and challenging, that have unfolded. Consider the ways you would like to continue to grow in the year ahead. In order to keep growing and flourishing throughout life – mentally, emotionally or spiritually – it's essential to keep an open mind and be willing to keep learning from and adapting to new situations. Part of this is assessing and accepting what is best for you to continue to nurture and support, and what is best to now gently let go of – just as many plants shed their flowers and leaves in the winter to allow for renewed growth and blossoming in spring. So here's to continued growth and new beginnings as we end this year and approach 2022...

AFFIRMATION OF THE MONTH

I am always growing in a range of ways

NOVEMBER 29 – DECEMBER 5
Growth

29 / MONDAY	30 / TUESDAY	1 / WEDNESDAY
	St Andrew's Day	World AIDS Day

NOTES

> "I want to be as idle as I can, so that
> my soul may have time to grow."

ELIZABETH VON ARNIM (1866–1941), BRITISH NOVELIST

2 / THURSDAY   3 / FRIDAY   4 / SATURDAY ●

5 / SUNDAY

EMBRACE IDLENESS

With so much to do, we often feel that idleness
is a luxury we can't afford. But idle moments
provide opportunities to ponder things we
might otherwise overlook. Spend up to one
hour this week without any distractions. Sit
outside or inside your favourite place in your
home and do absolutely nothing.

DECEMBER 6 – DECEMBER 12
Growth

6 / MONDAY

7 / TUESDAY

8 / WEDNESDAY
Bodhi Day (Buddha's Enlightenment) in some countries

NOTES

> ### "The risk to remain tight in a bud was more painful than the risk it took to blossom."
>
> ANAÏS NIN (1903–1977), FRENCH AUTHOR

9 / THURSDAY

10 / FRIDAY

11 / SATURDAY 》

----

12 / SUNDAY

IDENTIFY WHERE GROWTH IS NEEDED

Sometimes we need to grow even when we don't particularly want to. This week choose one aspect of your life – your career, your friendships, your romantic relationship, your emotional state – and ask yourself what three things you could do to help it grow and flourish in the future.

DECEMBER 13 – DECEMBER 19
Growth

13 / MONDAY	14 / TUESDAY	15 / WEDNESDAY

NOTES

> ## "What makes night within us may leave stars."

VICTOR HUGO (1802–1885), FRENCH WRITER

16 / THURSDAY   17 / FRIDAY   18 / SATURDAY

---

19 / SUNDAY ○

LOOK FOR THE SHINING STARS

Without dark we wouldn't be able to see the
beauty of the stars. Reflect on a difficult
situation you've experienced this year. List
three lessons you've learned from it. Note how
these helped you to grow as a person. Remind
yourself to look for the stars in your experience
the next time you find yourself in the dark.

DECEMBER 20 – DECEMBER 26
Growth

20 / MONDAY	21 / TUESDAY ♑	22 / WEDNESDAY
	Winter Solstice (UK, ROI, CAN, USA)	
	Summer Solstice (AUS, NZ)	

NOTES

"Always look for ways to nurture your dreams."

LAO TZU (FL. 6TH CENTURY BCE), CHINESE PHILOSOPHER

23 / THURSDAY

24 / FRIDAY
Christmas Eve

25 / SATURDAY
Christmas Day

26 / SUNDAY
Boxing Day / St Stephen's Day
Kwanzaa begins

NURTURE THE GROWTH OF YOUR DREAMS

Every day, visualize a dream becoming a reality. You're dreaming of a new house? What does it look like? Every day add an extra dimension. Perhaps your dream house has three bedrooms and a sea view. The more you picture it, the more you open your heart to it coming true.

DECEMBER 27 – JANUARY 2
Growth

27 / MONDAY ☾	28 / TUESDAY	29 / WEDNESDAY

NOTES

> ## "If we don't change, we don't grow.
> ## If we don't grow, we aren't really living."

ANATOLE FRANCE (1844–1924), FRENCH POET

30 / THURSDAY	31 / FRIDAY	1 / SATURDAY
	New Year's Eve	New Year's Day
		Kwanzaa ends

2 / SUNDAY ●

LOOK FORWARD TO THE FUTURE

Change is essential for growth. You've already changed so much in life for the better. This week, harness that positive, transformative energy and consider what more changes you would like to come. At the end of the week, write a list of five things you would like to change in your life in 2022.

DECEMBER OVERVIEW

M	TU	W	TH	F	SA	SU
29	30	1	2	3	4	5
6	7	8	9	10	11	12
13	14	15	16	17	18	19
20	21	22	23	24	25	26
27	28	29	30	31	1	2

This month I am grateful for . . .

Reflections on GROWTH

In what ways do you feel you have experienced the most growth this month, or year?

_____

_____

_____

_____

_____

_____

How did it feel to focus your attention on the theme of growth in your life?

_____

_____

_____

_____

_____

Are there any specific areas of your life that you'd like to focus on in the coming year when it comes to growth?

_____

_____

_____

_____

_____

INSPIRED JOURNALLING

The journalling pages that follow will encourage you to spend a little time reflecting on some of the things that many people hold dear, which will hopefully inspire you to pursue some of your own goals as you move through the year.

Each of the six pages corresponds to one of the monthly themes in the main diary and gives you space to make a personalized list – of places you'd like to visit, things you love about yourself, self-care ideas, films and shows you'd like to watch, what gives you joy, and books you'd like to read.

Just write down as few or as many ideas as they come into your mind under each theme. And, remember, you can come back to these lists and add to them any time you want, and indeed continue them elsewhere if you'd like, so just use them as will best benefit you...

Places I'd Like To Visit

CURIOSITY (JANUARY)

Travelling to new places, whether nearby or far off, is one of the most effective ways to stay curious and gain a healthy, new perspective on things, whether visiting a local park or museum that you've never been to before, a different town or city, or an entirely new country.

While there might not necessarily be big outings on the cards every week, there's no reason not to contemplate places you'd like to visit in the future. So take a little time out to think about some trips you'd really love to make and use the space below to make a list of these so that you can choose from them when you're ready to go!

Things I Love About Me

LOVING KINDNESS (APRIL)

It's all too easy to focus on giving love to others yet forgetting to give ourselves much love. So now's a chance to spend a little time nurturing ourselves a bit more, in the hope of developing more self-acceptance and self-love.

Sit somewhere quiet and allow yourself to identify and write down some things about yourself that you love. Nothing is too small or too large, from the colour of your eyes to the value that you place on family. There's no right or wrong answer here. It can feel uncomfortable – and maybe even difficult – to praise yourself at first, but the space below is a place for you to go to town, without fear of judgment or criticism!

Self-Care Ideas (for bad days)

STRENGTH (JULY)

Every time we're kind to ourselves, we're giving ourselves a well-deserved treat that helps to strengthen our reserves of energy and therefore makes us better able to cope with everything that life throws at us.

Use the space below to make a list of things that you could do to help yourself feel more nurtured and empowered from the inside out, whether this is making yourself a delicious fruit smoothie, taking a nice relaxing bath, calling an old friend who you've been meaning to phone for ages, or anything else that will help to recharge your batteries.

_____

_____

_____

_____

_____

_____

_____

_____

_____

_____

_____

_____

[Even if things are going well for you at the moment (yay!), these ideas will come into their own when you have a bad day in the future and aren't thinking straight, as you'll simply be able to flip back to this page and draw on the suggestions to start to make yourself feel better.]

Films & Shows I'd Like To Watch

CONNECTION (SEPTEMBER)

Television and film often get a bad rap as things we overindulge in, but there can be great value in taking a break from the real world now and again by diving into a show or film that reconnects you with a long-held passion, your emotional side, your sense of humour, your innate creativity, your inner child or any other part of yourself that tends not to be dominant in everyday life.

Use the space below to list some films and/or shows that you like the idea of tuning into – to the above end. Feel free to make a few separate lists if you prefer, based on, for example, shorter or longer viewing options, or maybe mood.

What Gives Me Joy

JOY (NOVEMBER)

Spending a little time reflecting on the things, people and experiences that bring us the most joy in life has the power not only to enhance our sense of appreciation and gratitude for life, but can also give us good insight into what matters most to us and what we might therefore want to incorporate more of into our lives.

So use the space below to list the things that make you feel amazing from the inside out, whether you experience this as a sense of calm and contentment, lightness and freedom, excitement and elation, a twinkle in your eye, or whatever else.

Books I'd Like To Read

GROWTH (DECEMBER)

Every time we read, we have the capacity to grow on an emotional level. Regardless of genre, books show us the world from new points of view and can help to open our minds and hearts to different ways of thinking and living.

Inspire yourself to cultivate more personal growth by jotting down in the space below some books you'd like to create time to read. If you can't think of any off hand, take this opportunity to do some research, whether online or in bookstores, into what genres, topics and approaches most float your boat.

Notes

Don't miss out on next year's diary!

To pre-order your 2022 *Every Day Matters Diary* from
September 2021 with FREE postage and packing,*
call our UK distributor on +44 (0)1206 255800.

*Free postage and packing for UK delivery addresses only. Offer limited to 3 books per order.

WATKINS
Sharing Wisdom Since 1893

Our books celebrate conscious, passionate, wise and happy living.
Be part of the community by visiting
watkinspublishing.com

  WatkinsPublishing   @watkinswisdom

WatkinsPublishingLtd   +watkinspublishing1893